CHELSEA MANNING

The Scandalous True Story of an All-American Whistleblower

Phil Coleman

Copyright © 2017.

All rights reserved. No part of this publication may be reproduced, distributed, or transmitted in any form or by any means, including photocopying, recording, or other electronic or mechanical methods, without the prior written permission of the publisher, except in the case of brief quotations embodied in critical reviews and certain other noncommercial uses permitted by copyright law.

This book is intended for informational and entertainment purposes only. The publisher limits all liability arising from this work to the fullest extent of the law.

Table of Contents

Leaked

Growing Up

Be All That You Can Be

Mental Health

Contact with Hackers

Response

The Secrets She Shared

Iceland Deal

Collateral Murder

War Logs

Diplomatic Cables

Guantanamo Bay Files

Granai Airstrike

Detention

Court Proceedings

Transitioning

Free Chelsea

Today

Leaked

The information came as a slow trickle. The whistleblower website WikiLeaks was just four years old, and the media didn't necessarily pay much attention to it. But then it came, the publication of a diplomatic cable on February 18, 2010. It was from the US embassy in Iceland's capitol city, Reykjavik, and detailed information about the country's financial crisis.

Two months later, a Wired report from April 5, 2010, screams with the headline, "Whistleblower Report: Leaked Video Shows U.S. 'Cover up,'" and said WikiLeaks founder Julian Assange called the course of the footage "courageous."

The Army's Criminal Investigative Division arrested the "courageous source" on May 26, 2010, and she was moved from Iraq to Camp Arifjan, Kuwait where she was held until July 6 without being charged. When the charges finally came, they were for violating the Uniform Code of Military Justice because she had transferred classified information to a personal computer and added unauthorized software to a classified computer.

All of the actions violated federal laws about the handling of classified information.

Who had access to that volume of information? Why did they do it? Where was the leak coming from?

Growing Up

Chelsea was born Bradley Edward Manning on December 17, 1987, in Oklahoma City, Oklahoma. She was the youngest child by more than a decade. Her sister, Casey, was born in 1976.

Chelsea's father, Brian, was a Navy man who met Susan Fox, a Welsh woman, while he was stationed in Wales in the mid-1970s. Brian was an intelligence analyst for five years. The couple moved with Casey back to California in 1979. It wasn't long before they made the move to Crescent, Oklahoma, about half an hour north of Oklahoma, City. They had a small, five-acre hobby farm with cows and chickens and a two-story home.

Brian transitioned to a job at the Hertz Corporation where he managed computer programmers. Susan stayed home, though Chelsea's sister Casey testified in later court hearings that both parents were alcoholics, and Susan was unable to function. Instead, Casey cared for her infant brother, who was later left to his own devices. An Army psychologist would later say Chelsea exhibited some physical symptoms of fetal alcohol syndrome.

In 2010, Chelsea confided in Adrian Lamo that she began working on computers and could read and do advanced math before she even began school. Chelsea described herself as an "easy target" by kindergarten and suffered from taunting, often hearing "girly boy" and "teacher's pet" hurled at him.

At home, Chelsea read the encyclopedia, watched PBS, played with Lego bricks and tinkered with Brian's old computers. The family was Catholic, though Chelsea later said she never believed a word of it.

"Always been too intellectual, if not just plain queer, for religion," she told Lamo.

She described her mother as nice but emotionally needy. She described Brian as abusive and lamented the isolation she felt growing up because their home was isolated enough they had no close neighbors.

Chelsea was bright; she was a three-time winner of the town science fair and participated in an academic bowl team.

As elementary school neared the end and Chelsea went into middle school, her peers began calling her "gay." Chelsea, who self-described herself as "effeminate" as a child, told Lamo that she "didn't know what gay meant, but knew it was something bad."

To combat it, Chelsea joined sports teams and began trying to become athletic.

A drunken fight with her armed father was the catalyst that blew Chelsea's world apart.

She told Lamo she was doing "noisy homework" one night and interrupted Brian's television show.

Like most nights, Brian was drunk and grew angry. According to Chelsea, Brian got a shotgun from his bedroom and chased her out of the house. The deadbolt on the door slowed Chelsea down and Brian caught up to her, which prompted Susan (also intoxicated) to smash a lamp over Brian's head.

Chelsea fought her father, breaking his nose before she ran out of the house.

Brian fired his shotgun and Chelsea was beat with a belt for "making him shoot up the house."

Finally, at school the next day, the teachers got social workers involved. Susan filed for divorce, but attempted suicide in 1998.

Two years later, Brian married a second woman named Susan and his new stepson took the Manning name—a move that reportedly greatly upset Chelsea.

In 2001, Chelsea left with Susan and the two returned to her hometown in Wales where he attended Tasker Milward School for high school. The bullying continued because she was the only American and was still picked on for having more feminine qualities.

Around 2005, when Chelsea was 17, Susan grew ill and had a couple strokes. Chelsea decided she wanted to go home to the US and travelled to London in July of 2005 to get her passport renewed.

Back in the states, she didn't stay in any one place for very long. She went home to Brian in Oklahoma City. Brian told PBS's Frontline that she was "spoiled rotten" when she returned from Europe and didn't get along Brian's new wife.

A fight about house rules got out of hand on March 29, 2006, and police ended up removing Chelsea from the home without arresting her. Chelsea left for Tulsa the next day.

In Tulsa, she worked for a pizza joint and for an FYE store. Eventually she headed to Chicago to work at a Guitar Center.

She finally moved to her aunt's home where she worked two jobs—Starbucks and

Abercrombie and Fitch — while attending community college.

Be All That You Can Be

Chelsea testified in 2013 that she chose to go to basic training because she wanted to go to take advantage of the GI Bill and go to college. She'd taken the Armed Services Aptitude Battery test and scored high enough to take an enlisted position.

When she told her recruiter she was interested in IT work and geopolitical matters, the recruiter suggested she become an intelligence analyst, the same work her father had done with the Navy in the 1970s.

"In particular, I enjoyed the fact that an analyst would use information derived from a variety of sources to create work products that informed the command on its available choices for determining the best courses of action. Although the MOS required a working knowledge of computers, it primarily required me to consider how raw information can be combined with other available intelligence sources in order to create products that assisted the command in its situational awareness," Chelsea said in her statement.

She reported to Fort Leonard Wood on Oct. 2, 2007, for basic training.

Basic training proved very difficult for Chelsea. She told the court that she wasn't physically or mentally prepared for the requirements. It took her six months to complete the training instead of the typical 10 weeks.

She'd injured her right shoulder and left foot and was placed on medical hold. Her superior officers considered processing her out, but she resisted; she believed she could get through the injuries. She still felt different from the other soldiers. A fellow recruit later told Wired magazine that Chelsea was taunted and often called a "faggot." At five-foot, two-inches tall, she'd have likely been the smallest recruit there.

Chelsea started basic training over on Jan. 20, 2008, completed training on April 2 of that year, and reported for intelligence analyst training on April 7 at Fort Huachuca, Arizona.

Chelsea said the training was enjoyable and she felt as if she fit in with her peers. She felt there was purpose and use in reviewing information to "actionable products."

It was also at Fort Huachuca that she first learned of WikiLeaks.

In August 2008, Chelsea reported to Fort Drum, New York, her first official duty station. Her job had her working with Significant Activities (SIGACTS).

SIGACTS, according to Chelsea, give a first impression of an event. That event could be when soldiers encounter IED attacks or engage in small arms fire with hostile forces. Once an event is reported, it is then passed up the chain of command from brigade to division to corps and published in its final version at the corps level.

The non-commissioned-officer-in-charge noted her skills and asked her to work on the Incident Tracker, an abandoned program previously worked on by a former analyst.

She refined the Incident Tracker and used the SIGACTS from Afghanistan to populate it as her unit was set to deploy to Logar and Wardak provinces. When their orders changed and they were assigned to Baghdad, Iraq, she exchanged the Afghani SIGACTS for Iraqi SIGACTS.

Chelsea later told the court that she didn't believe an individual SIGACT was very sensitive because most of them contained information about engaging the enemy or casualties — both of which are widely reported. To her, most SIGACTs seemed like a daily journal.

Chelsea began seeing a man named Tyler Watkins, a Brandeis University student, while she was stationed at Fort Drum. Watkins introduced her to the hacker community in the area.

In September 2009, she spent four weeks at the Joint Readiness Training Center at Fort Polk, Louisiana, and her unit arrived at Forward Operating Base Hammer outside of Baghdad in October 2009.

While she'd known of WikiLeaks while in training at Fort Huachuca, nothing caught her eye about it until she'd already arrived in Iraq.

"I did not full pay attention until WLO (WikiLeaks organization) released purported short messaging system (SMS/text) messages from 11 September 2001 on 25 November 2009," Chelsea said in her statement.

At that point, she began researching WikiLeaks and monitoring the website. She also monitored news reports and private intelligence agencies for more information.

"This practice was something I was trained to do during AIT, and it was something that good analysts are expected to do," she said in the statement.

WikiLeaks actually proved useful to Chelsea. Her statement to the court recounted using information at the site that was integrated into some of her work products.

She also became involved with WikiLeaks chat threads between people using the WikiLeaks side.

"Initially, I simply observed the IRC conversations. I wanted to know how the organization was structured, and how they obtained their data. The conversations I viewed were usually technical in nature, but sometimes switched to a lively debate on issues a particular individual felt strongly about," Her statement said.

But her interest was piqued. She found herself involved in the chats when the topic turned to computers or world events. At times, WikiLeaks seemed academic to her.

In early January 2010, she took a CD-RW labeled "Lady Gaga" and burned a copy of SIGACTS from both Iraq and Afghanistan.

"At the time I did so, I did not intent to use this information for any purpose other than for back-up. However, I later decided to release this information publicly. At that time I believed, and still believe, that these tables are two of the most significant documents of our time," her statement said.

She later told hacker Adrian Lamo that she'd listened to and lip synced along to Lady Gaga's Telephone while "exfiltrating possible the biggest data spillage in American history."

It was almost time for Chelsea's mid-tour leave, and she decided she would save the documents to her laptop and her camera's SD card and take them home to figure out what to do with them.

Her leave began on January 23, 2010, and she found herself at her aunt's home in Potomac, Maryland. She made immediate plans to see her boyfriend, Tyler, but found that their relationship had cooled significantly. She had wanted to ask Tyler what he'd do if he was sitting on a treasure trove of information, but Tyler didn't have a specific answer.

"I began feeling that I was overstaying my welcome, and I returned to Maryland. I spent the remainder of my time on leave in the Washington, D.C. area," the statement said.

It was during leave that she made the decision to go into public as a woman for the first time.

Chelsea donned a wig, make up, and a business casual clothing to venture around the city. He later told hacker Adrian Lamo that it came naturally.

"Instead of thinking all the time about how I'm perceived, being self-conscious, I just let myself go… … well I was still self-conscious, but in a different way…I was worried about whether I looked pretty, whether my makeup was running, whether I spilled coffee on my (expensive) outfit…and to some extent whether I was passing…" she typed to Lamo one afternoon before her arrest.

The New York Times called her jaunt around the city as a woman as the highlight of the two-week leave.

A blizzard stranded her at her aunt's home for several days where she had time to think about the data she'd brought back. Before she returned to the Middle East, she decided she had to share it.

"I felt we were risking so much for people that seemed unwilling to cooperate with us, leading to frustration and hatred on both sides…" she said in her statement. "…In attempting to conduct counter-terrorism and counter-insurgency operations, we became obsessed with capturing and killing human targets on lists, on being suspicious of and avoiding cooperation with our host-nation partners, and ignoring the second and third order effects of accomplishing short-term goals and missions."

Chelsea believed releasing the data could spark a debate about America's foreign policy as it related to Iraq and Afghanistan.

"At that point, I decided it made sense to try and disclose the SIGACT tables to an American Newspaper," she said.

First she called the Washington Post, but the reporter there didn't seem interested, saying that the data would have to be reviewed and then senior editors would have to consider the content.

She tried the New York Times as well and called the number for the public editor listed on the website. She got an answering machine and left her Skype name and email address but never heard back.

She kicked around taking the information to Politico, but winter weather kept her in Maryland.

She circled back around to WikiLeaks.

"I ultimately decided I would submit the materials to the WLO. I was not sure if WLO would actually publish the SIGACT tables, or, even if they did publish, I was concerned they might not be noticed by the American media. However, based on what I read about WLO through my research...this seemed to be the best medium for publishing this information to the world within my reach," she said in her statement.

She joined another WikiLeaks chatroom and said she had information that needed to be shared with the world. Another user quickly linked her to the submission system for the site.

Finally, on February 3, 2010, Chelsea used the link and submitted all of the Iraq and

Afghan SIGACTS to WikiLeaks. She included a statement in a text file that she'd hoped to share with the Washington Post.

"Items of historical significance of two wars Iraq and Afghanistan Significant Activity, Sigacts, between 0001 January 2004 and 2359 31 December 2009 extracts from CSV documents from Department of Defense and CDNE database.

These items have already been sanitized of any source identifying information.

You might need to sit on this information for 90 to 180 days to best send and distribute such a large amount of data to a large audience and protect the source.

This is one of the most significant documents of our time removing the fog of war and revealing the true nature of 21st century asymmetric warfare.

Have a good day," it said.

Chelsea was back at FOB Hammer on February 11, 2010. The information from her data dump had not appeared on WikiLeaks yet, but she told the court that she felt a sense of relief and had a clear conscience because she'd exposed what was happening in Iraq and Afghanistan.

Mental Health

Chelsea didn't adjust very well to Army life and was often in trouble for outbursts, being late, and fighting.

A memorandum in the court file dated May 8, 2010, just a few weeks prior to her arrèst, outlines an incident that happened around 6:30 p.m. the night before.

She left a meal with other soldiers and was found on the floor of a storage room curled into the fetal position.

The master sergeant, Paul Adkins, who went to check on her found her clutching her head with his eyes shut. The words "I WANT" had been carved into a folding chair and an open knife lay at her feet.

The master sergeant talked at length with Chelsea, who said she didn't feel like she was a person, that she had no personality. "(She) drew the analogy of (her) being a turtle with a core personality and several layers of hardened shell, fragmented and designed to protect the core personality, and function in different situations as the need required," the master sergeant wrote.

She reportedly fluctuated between calm and "in pain," according to the document. Adkins felt comfortable sending her to finish the last four hours of her shift, but she ended up in a physical altercation with a female soldier.

When Adkins spoke with her after she struck the other soldier, Adkins said that he and Chelsea talked at length about why she joined the army and her childhood. Chelsea was reportedly concerned about the ramifications of her actions, afraid that she'd receive an other-than-honorable discharge.

Adkins wrote a longer statement on June 10, 2010, with more details about the troubled soldier.

That statement, which was not admitted into evidence, said that she showed signs of mental instability as early as 2009 when she had a negative reaction to counseling.

The army counseled her several times in 2009 for various infractions such as failure to report and disrespect.

"Your excessive caffeine consumption is a possible hindrance to your overall performance as it may be hindering your rest cycle and hydration impacting your overall performance," her counselor wrote in her initial April 2009 counseling session.

Chelsea reportedly overslept and missed a 7 a.m. report time for an accountability formation. When she was woken up and brought to the formation, she reportedly became so enraged, she began screaming and shaking with her fists clenched, according to the report. Her previous initials, "BEM" are visible on the report. At that time, the report threatened her with discharge for future failures. In addition, she was ordered to report to morning formation at 5:40 a.m. instead of 7 a.m.

Two months later, Chelsea appeared to be adjusting to military life a bit better according to the counseling report.

She was congratulated for completing analyst training, but her physical fitness was still considered a weakness.

There were some issues alluded to but not outlined in the report. "While TDY at school there were some accusations and conflicts," it read.

Adkins believed counseling would help Chelsea, and higher-ranking soldiers had discussed leaving her behind when they deployed to Iraq because of her issues.

Within a few weeks of getting to Iraq in fall of 2009, she got in touch with a gender counselor in the United States to say she felt female and isolated because the military's "Don't ask, don't tell" policy was still in full force. Had she been open about her sexuality and status as a trans-woman, she'd have risked dishonorable discharge.

On April 24, 2010, three weeks after the Collateral Murder video was released, Chelsea sent an email with the subject "My Problem" to Adkins. She attached a photo of herself as a woman. The photo was named breanna.jpg. At the time, she was referring to herself as Breanna. She told her supervisor she was suffering from gender identity disorder.

"This is my problem. I've had signs of it for a very long time. It's caused problems within my family. I thought a career in the military would get rid of it. It's not something I seek out for attention, and I've been trying very, very hard to get rid of it by placing myself in situations where it would be impossible," she wrote. "But, it's not going away; it's haunting me more and more as I get older. Now, the consequences of it are dire, at a time when it's causing me great pain in itself.

Adkins never passed the information any higher up the chain of command. After

Chelsea's arrest, Adkins had to answer for his failure to report the email.

"Under no circumstances should we have allowed him to continue to perform his duties as an intelligence analyst," Adkins' superior officer said in part. "...I honestly do not know what I would have done to PFC Manning if I were in your situation. However, I would haves sought guidance from the chain of command."

Adkins later told the court martial that he was worried the photograph would have been circulated among the other soldiers had he sought help from the higher-ups.

In 2011, her counselor told New York Magazine that she was clearly in a crisis when she reached out. She didn't fit in with the other soldiers, and her shifts consisted of working in tight, dimly lit quarters for up to 15 hours at a time.

Contact with Hackers

WikiLeaks is a platform that anonymously publishes leaked data from anonymous sources. Its domain, www.wikileaks.org, was first registered in October 2006. It was the brainchild of Australian Julian Assange.

Assange is a 46-year-old computer programmer and award winning journalist.

The first leaked document — approval to kill Somali government officials by Somalian politician Hassan Dahir Aweys — was posted to the site in December 2006.

By summer 2007, news outlets were beginning to use WikiLeaks as a source in reporting, though it wasn't until Chelsea's arrest that WikiLeaks became a household name.

Chelsea had been watching the WikiLeaks chatrooms prior to dumping the data, but after she released the Collateral Murder video, she began chatting with another WikiLeaks user under the handle, "office."

Chelsea said in her statement that she believed the person was a higher up at WikiLeaks, but the two never exchanged any personally identifiable information. Eventually, Chelsea named the person "Nathaniel Frank" in her address book.

It is now believed that Nathaniel Frank could have been Julian Assange himself.

Chelsea was loose with the information, telling at least two people in May 2010 that she was the source of the Collateral Murder video.

On May 9, she reached out to Jonathan Odell, a Minesota novelist. She reportedly told him she played a part in "very high-profile events, albeit as a nameless individual thus far."

On May 19, Chelsea emailed Eric Schmiedl, a mathematician from Boston. A PDF of that exchange is available in the court documents.

"Are you familiar with Wikileaks?" Chelsea asked.

"Yeah, I am," Schmiedl answered back.

"I was the source of the 12 July 2007 video from the Apache Weapons Team, which killed the two journalists and injured the two kids," Chelsea replied.

Chelsea also reached out to Adrian Lamo, a hacker who was arrested for breaking into computer networks at Microsoft, Yahoo!, and the New York Times. Lamo had been arrested in September 2003 for the hack and later sentenced to six months of house arrest, two years of probation, and he had to pay $65,000 in restitution.

Lamo's sworn testimony was sealed on August 20, 2013, but chat logs of the several-day conversation he had with Chelsea were released by Wired magazine in 2011.

Lamo and Chelsea had talked at length about her life and sexuality. On May 22, 2010, Chelsea was chatting with Lamo, lamenting her status with the army and the isolation she felt as a "super intelligent, awkwardly effeminate supply guy."

"I'm in the desert, with a bunch of hyper-masculine trigger happy rednecks as neighbors...and the only safe place I seem to have is the satellite internet connection," she wrote. "And I already got myself into minor trouble, revealing my uncertainty over my gender identity...which is causing me to lose this job...putting me in an awkward limbo."

Within an hour, she was discussing classified information with Lamo.

"Hypothetical question: if you had free reign over classified networks for long periods of time... say, 8-9 months... and you saw incredible things, awful things... things that belonged in the public domain, and not on some server stored in a dark room in Washington DC... what would you do?" Chelsea asked the hacker.

She continued to allude to her actions, telling Lamo that "someone" she knew had been mining data and "uploading it to a crazy white-haired Aussie who can't seem to stay in one country very long."

She then went on to say, "I've made a huge mess."

Chelsea told Lamo it was important the information get out, and she said she wasn't even afraid to spend the rest of her life in prison or even be executed, but she didn't want to be seen as a male when her face was inevitably plastered on newspapers and television screens.

Lamo asked a few questions of her, and Chelsea was explicit about the role she was playing— "but I'm not a source for you… I'm talking to you as someone who needs moral and emotional fucking support," she wrote.

Lamo was supportive, offering digital hugs to Chelsea and telling her she could still rebuild her life.

She told Lamo more about what finally caused her to start looking at the world differently before she started leaking information was a video of 15 detainees who were captured by the Iraqi Federal Police for printing "anti-Iraqi literature."

"The Iraqi federal police wouldn't cooperate with US forces, so I was instructed to investigate the matter, find out who the "bad guys" were, and how significant this was for the FPs (federal police)... it turned out, they had printed a scholarly critique against PM (prime minister) (Nouri al) Maliki... I had an interpreter read it for me... and when I found out that it was a benign political critique titled "Where did the money go?" and following the corruption trail within the PM's cabinet... I immediately took that information and ran to the officer to explain what was going on… he didn't want to hear any of it… he told me to shut up and explain how we could assist the FPs in finding more detainees," Chelsea told Lamo. "Everything started slipping after that… I saw things differently. I had always questioned the things worked, and investigated to find the truth… but that was a point where I was a part of something… I was actively involved in something that I was completely against…

Lamo took the information he had to the authorities, yet it seemed like he tried to warn her.

A report from Wired Magazine in 2011 said that Lamo contacted some friends about Chelsea's leak on May 21 and was eventually in touch with the Army's Criminal Investigation Division. Lamo later testified in court that he turned her in because he was worried lives were in danger.

Still, after he'd turned Chelsea in, Lamo asked her what she'd do if her cover was blown.

"Try and figure out how I could get my side of the story out... before everything was twisted around to make me look like Nidal Hassan," she replied.

Nidal Hassan is an American soldier convicted of killing 13 people and wounding more than 30 others in a mass shooting at Fort Hood, Texas, on Nov. 5, 2009.

Chelsea wasn't worried she'd be detected, and it was obvious in the chat logs that he explicitly trusted Lamo. She told Lamo she was regularly ignored while on the job and said the network was so cobbled together there'd be no way to trace her.

"I'd be one paranoid boy in your shoes," Lamo warned.

Lamo also asked Chelsea who he should talk to if she disappeared.

Response

The data trickling out of WikiLeaks and the information from the Army about who was responsible was the topic of wall-to-wall media coverage. Governments were left scrambling to block their citizens from seeing embarrassing diplomatic information. The editor of the Guardian said he couldn't think of another time when the entire world was talking about a single event that wasn't a war or terrorist attack.

Other members of the military had harsh words for Chelsea, accusing her of putting US servicemen and their Afghan informants in mortal danger. President Obama was caught on camera saying she'd broken the law.

Some analysts credited Chelsea's data dump with kicking off the Arab Spring that began in December 2010.

The Washington Post penned an editorial asking why an Army private in a mental health crisis had access to a massive trove of sensitive materials.

A year after the breach, the Department of Defense found that there'd been no significant harm done by the data dump. This report, however, was kept a secret until she had already been released from prison.

In late June 2017, Mike Pompeo, director of the CIA, told the Associated Press that he believes the release of sensitive information is on the rise because of how many people admire people like Edward Snowden, a former CIA employee who disclosed information about surveillance programs, and Chelsea.

The Secrets She Shared

In all, Chelsea took more than 700,000 documents on a myriad of topics ranging from information about war maneuvers to diplomatic relations to conditions in Guantanamo Bay, Cuba.

Iceland Deal

After hearing about something in Iceland via the WikiLeaks chat room, Chelsea went searching through government databases in early January 2010 to see if she could learn anything. At that time there was no information.

By the time she returned from her mid-tour leave, the topic was referenced in government databases. The two-page cable had been published on January 13.

"I read the cable, and quickly concluded that Iceland was essentially being bullied, diplomatically, by two larger European powers. It appeared to me that Iceland was out of viable solutions, and was now coming to the U.S. for assistance. Despite their quiet request for assistance, it did not appear we were going to do anything. From my perspective, it appeared we were not getting involved due to the lack of long term geopolitical benefit to do so."

At this point, WikiLeaks hadn't published anything she'd provided from the SIGACT data, so she again copied the information to a CD and put it on her personal laptop to upload it to WikiLeaks.

This time, her submission was published within hours.

Collateral Murder

In mid-February 2010, she overheard some fellow soldiers talking about a video on a drive. That video depicted an air weapons team engaging with several individuals, eventually killing a dozen people. At first, Chelsea thought nothing off the video; it looked like all the other videos of combat she'd seen.

It was the audio, however, that deeply troubled her.

The other people in the room began debating whether or not the crew had violated rules of engagement.

Chelsea told the police that she'd shied away from the debate, instead searching for information online by searching for information from the date from the video: July 12, 2007.

Google returned results for news accounts detailing two Reuter's journalists who were killed that day by an air weapons team. Reuters had filed a Freedom of Information Act request to see the video, hoping to learn what had gone wrong so they could protect other journalists embedded in war zones.

At the time, the Army's central command told Reuters that they weren't sure the video still existed and couldn't provide a timeline for when they might even consider the FOIA request.

Chelsea found a second story from a year later that reported Reuters was still pursuing its request though the Army had still never provided a formal response to their inquiry.

The bloodshed and implications on the tape's audio troubled her deeply.

"It was clear to me that the event happened because the air weapons team mistakenly identified the Reuters employees with a potential threat, and that the people in the bongo truck were merely attempting to assist the wounded. The people in the van were not a threat, but 'good Samaritans,'" her statement said.

The video depicted a seriously wounded individual on the ground attempting to crawl to safety. "Instead of calling for medical attention to the location, one of the air weapons team crew members verbally asked for the wounded person to pick up a weapon so he would have a reason to engage," she said.

Next, the bongo truck approached to aid the wounded person. The air weapons team then fires on the truck. When an infantry unit arrives at the scene, the air team learns there were children in the van and downplayed what had happened, saying, "well it's their fault for bringing their kids into a battle."

Chelsea's statement said she was alarmed by the "delightful bloodlust" shown by the air weapons team.

"They dehumanized the individuals they were engaging, and seemed to not value human life by referring to them as "dead bastards" and congratulating each other on the ability to kill in large numbers."

On February 15, 2010 — the same day she made copies of the Iceland cable — Chelsea copied the video of the air weapons team shooting the journalists and other relevant documents to a CD and placed it on her personal laptop.

She had planned on hanging on to the information until she got home from her tour in September 2010, but changed her mind when she realized WikiLeaks printed the Icelandic document. On February 21, she submitted the video to WikiLeaks as well and notified the individuals in the WikiLeaks chatroom about what he'd done.

"I wanted the American public to know that not everyone in Iraq and Afghanistan were targets that needed to be neutralized, but rather people who were struggling to live in the 'pressure-cooker; environment of what we call asymmetric warfare," her statement said.

WikiLeaks published the video on April 5, 2010.

According to a story from the Guardian that same day, the video couldn't have come at a worse time — the Army had just admitted some special forces members attempted to cover up the killing of three Afghan women by removing the bullets from their bodies.

According to the Guardian, the military initially claimed the helicopters were responding to an active firefight and had killed a dozen insurgents.

War Logs

At the end of July 2010, while Chelsea was still held in Kuwait, Wikileaks, along with three other news organizations, began publishing almost 100,000 documents about the Afghan War. The documents contained information from a six-year span that touched on allegations of foreign support for the Taliban, Al-Qaeda, informants, psychological warfare, child prostitution, civilian and friendly fire casualties at the hands of American soldiers, as well as insurgent attacks. This information became known as the Afghan War Logs.

In October 2010, Wikileaks published almost 400,000 documents that became known as the Iraq War Logs.

The Iraq War logs purported to show many abuses at the hands of Americans while in Iraq including 15,000 unreported civilian deaths, the murder of Iraqis attempting to surrender, and the death of hundreds of people simply because they came too close to checkpoints.

Diplomatic Cables

The leak of 250,000 state department cables dating from 1966 to 2010 began appearing on WikiLeaks in November 2010. It became known as "Cablegate" in the media. It was the largest leak of confidential documents in history.

Most of the cables dealt with political relations or external affairs, but they also touched on terrorism, the UN Security Council, human rights and economic conditions. The cables had been written by embassies and consulates in 180 countries. The dump reportedly caused one Ethiopian journalist to leave his country, and the US said it had to relocate several source for their protection.

Guantanamo Bay Files

The Guantanamo Bay files were released by WikiLeaks and published in the New York Times on April 24, 2011. The 779 documents — classified as secret — related to prisoners and the living conditions at the detention facility in Guantanamo Bay, Cuba. The island prison was established by America in 2002 following the invasion of Afghanistan in response to the terror attacks on September 11, 2001.

The Times reported more than 150 innocent people were among those detained in Cuba without being charged for years. Those prisoners included a 14-year-old boy and an 89-year-old man.

More than 100 inmates were diagnosed with mental illness, and the US reportedly tried to detain British residents. An Al Jazeera journalist spent four years in custody where he was questioned extensively about Al Jazeera operations. The journalist also said he had been beaten and assaulted as officials attempted to turn him into an informant.

Granai Airstrike

One of the videos she leaked was from a May 4, 2009, air strike that killed dozens of Afghan civilians in the village of Granai, Afghanistan. Estimates put the death toll anywhere between 86 and 146 people.

The US government later said there were significant errors as troops hadn't been able to properly differentiate between civilians and the enemy.

Though the video had been in WikiLeaks possession, it was never published. Assange said in a 2013 interview that a former WikiLeaks employee had taken the video and destroyed it when he left the organization.

Detention

Following her arrest and transfer to Kuwait Chelsea was locked in a steel cage that said "Made in Fort Wayne," according to a New York Times report from June 2017. She told the Times she felt isolated and was fairly certain it was Lamo who revealed her identity. She believed that her transmission to WikiLeaks had been in vain, that no one knew the truth and she'd still be locked away for life.

She had been able to get in touch with her aunt back in Maryland to ask her to post to her Facebook page for him, according to PBS Frontline

"Some of you may have heard that I have been arrested for disclosure of classified information to unauthorized persons. See http://collateralmurder.com," said a June 5, 2010 post on what was then the "Bradley Manning" Facebook page.

The URL was a link to the WikiLeaks page.

Later reports would detail instances of Chelsea's emotional trauma while being held in Kuwait... At times she would yell, scream, shake, and sometimes bang her head on the walls or mumble

After a week, she attempted to hang herself with her sheets. After a medical evaluation, she was diagnosed with "probable gender identity disorder" as well as anxiety and depression. The medicine to stop the anxiety made her ill.

In late July, a few days after WikiLeaks released the Afghan logs; she was loaded on a plane in shackles. The guards were unclear about where she'd be sent — at first they said a Navy cruiser, but then told her she'd be detained at Guantanamo Bay. Once the flight was in the air, they told her she'd be at the Marine brig at Quantico, Virginia.

In Virginia, she realized people knew who she was when a guard told her she was all over Fox News.

She was on "Prevention of Injury" status because officials believed she was a suicide risk. She didn't have clothes, instead wearing a smock that couldn't be turned into a rope to hang her. She had no bed clothes or pillows, and guards checked on her every few minutes. She was forced to remain awake between 5 a.m. and 8 p.m., and had to stand if she tried to doze off. She had zero privacy, and had to be visible to guards at all times.

Her cell at Quantico had no window, and she couldn't see any of the other detainees. She was only allowed out for a walk one hour per day. Her entertainment was limited to watching a television in the corridor or reading the single book and magazine she was allowed to keep. All meals were eaten in her cell and when she did have visitors, she remained shackled.

In January 2011, Chelsea was reportedly involved in an altercation with guards and later said the guards started issuing conflicting orders to get her into trouble. She was placed on suicide watch again and was forced to remain alone 24 hours a day without even her eyeglasses.

In March, the guards confiscated her underwear and made her sleep naked one night.

Eventually, outsiders learned of Chelsea's treatment while in custody, and her conditions were regarded by some as "illegal and immoral."

A United Nations rapporteur, Juan Mendez, was quoted in the Guardian as saying her treatment was "cruel, inhumane and degrading." Amnesty International became involved in the case because she was the descendent of a British woman. Even a US State Department employee criticized her treatment and was forced to resign two days later.

In April, a petition was signed by almost 300 American legal scholars arguing that the conditions Chelsea was enduring in the brig were a violation of the constitution.

Finally, at the end of April 2011, she was dropped into the general population at the Midwest Joint Regional Correctional Facility at Fort Leavenworth, Kansas. Her new cell had a window and a normal mattress, and she could again have personal objects and interact with other pretrial detainees. Fort Leavenworth was where she returned following her conviction in 2013.

The 515-bed maximum security complex was designed to house military prisoners with the longest sentences. Chelsea's second-floor cell was narrow, but it had a northward-facing window.

Despite announcing her gender identity as female following sentencing, she was still required to adhere to Army appearance regulations—and she was still addressed and treated as if she were male.

She requested the Army give her access to hormone therapy, but the Army refused, instead saying her treatment for gender identity issues would consist of antidepressants and counseling.

The Army held that stance for almost a year, until they finally agreed to allow Chelsea to have women's underwear in the summer of 2014. In early 2015, they finally started administering hormone therapy.

While in prison, she worked with the other inmates in the wood shop where they built furniture from scratch. She also played Dungeons and Dragons, assuming the role of a female character.

Journalists were not allowed to visit Chelsea; the only visitors permitted were the ones named before she'd been sentenced. No one was allowed to take her photo, and she couldn't give phone interviews, but she was allowed to read the news.

Chelsea sent a letter to Amnesty International telling them she was taking college classes for a bachelor's degree, working out, and staying up to date on current events.

Cosmopolitan reported that Chelsea was optimistic in early 2015 and said she'd made friends with inmates who didn't seem to be bothered that she identified as a woman.

Sometimes she wrote opinion pieces to the Guardian regarding her thoughts on world events and life in prison. Chelsea was reflective in a May 27, 2015, column in the Guardian.

She still defended her choice to release the documents, but reflected on the five years she'd already spend incarcerated.

"In 2010, I was considerably less mature than I am now, and the potential consequences and outcomes of my actions seemed vague and very surreal to me. I certainly expected the worst possible outcome, but I lacked a strong sense of what "the worst" would entail. I did expect to be demonized and targeted, to have every moment of my life re-examined and analyzed for every possible personal flaw and blemish, and to have them used against me in the court of public opinion or against transgender people as a whole," she wrote in part. "…It can be hard, sometimes, to make sense of all the things that have happened to me in the last five years (let alone my entire life). The things that seem consistent and clear to me are the support that I receive from my friends, my family and the millions of people all over the world. Through every struggle that I have been confronted with, and have been subjected to – solitary confinement, long legal battles and physically transitioning to the woman I have always been – I manage not only to survive, but to grow, learn, mature and thrive as a better, more confident person."

Court Proceedings

About the same time Chelsea was moved to Fort Leavenworth during her pretrial phase, a panel of experts finally ruled that she was fit to stand trial. It would still be eight months — a total of 19 months since her arrest — that she finally got her Article 32 hearing. Article 32 hearings are the military equivalent of a preliminary hearing.

Prosecutors presented 300,000 pages of documents as evidence, including classified material.

Army investigators testified that they found 400,000 military reports from Iraq, 91,000 from Afghanistan, 100,000 diplomatic cables and 10,000 miscellaneous cables stored in various places on Chelsea's work computer, her personal laptop, or the SD card she'd left in her aunt's basement during the mid-tour leave.

She had forgotten to delete some of her encrypted chats between herself and Nathaniel Frank/Julian Assange.

Investigators found that there had been two attempts to remove material from the laptop. The operating system had been reinstalled in January 2010, and there'd been an attempt to delete everything from the hard drive at the end of that month.

Following the December 16, 2011, hearing, the Lieutenant Colonel in charge recommended a court-martial. Chelsea was arraigned after two months, in February 2013, later but declined to enter a plea at that time.

There was some respite that winter — Colonel Denise Lind shaved 112 days off whatever sentence she received because of how she'd been treated at Quantico.

Chelsea did end up pleading guilty to 10 of the 22 charges against her. Prosecutors prepared to go ahead with the court-martial on the remaining charges.

Her court martial began on June 3, 2013 and continued through July 30. On the second day of the trial, Lamo and Chelsea came face to face during the proceedings.

According to the New York Times, Lamo agreed that he could see Chelsea really wanted to make the world a better place, but Lamo's concerns about safety prompted him to reach out to authorities. Chelsea reportedly listened intently, but didn't look at Lamo as he left the courtroom following about half an hour of testimony.

She was found guilty on 17 of the 22 charges, but was acquitted on the aiding the enemy charge.

During the weeks-long sentencing hearing, which began on July 31, two psychologists attempted to explain why she'd done it. An army psychologist told the court-martial that Chelsea showed signs of Asperger syndrome and had narcissistic traits. She said been "acting out a grandiose ideation" when she released the material.

The second psychiatrist said she wanted to "crowd source an analysis of the war"

Chelsea did address the court on April 14.

On August 14, she apologized to the court: "I am sorry that my actions hurt people. I'm sorry that they hurt the United States. I am sorry for the unintended consequences of my actions. When I made these decisions I believed I was going to help people, not hurt people. ... At the time of my decisions I was dealing with a lot of issues," she said.

She was facing 90 years in prison, and the government wanted her to serve 60. Her attorney, David Coombs, hoped she would receive less than 25.

The judge split the middle, sentencing her to 35 years in prison, a reduction in rank to private, a dishonorable discharge, and forfeiture of pay. She had credit for 1,293 days already served—including the 112 for her time at Quantico. She would have been eligible for parole after serving an additional eight years—for a total of 11.6 years behind bars.

The Guardian and the New York Times were immediately critical of her sentence, calling it "unjust and unfair" and "excessive.

There was the chance of a presidential pardon or commutation, but that seemed unlikely considering that the White House had condemned the leaks

Transitioning

The day after sentencing, Chelsea's attorney contacted NBC's Today show to announce that the soldier everyone had known as Bradley Edward Manning was actually female, and would prefer to be known as Chelsea Elizabeth Manning with female pronouns.

Her attorney included a statement from Chelsea in his release.

"As I transition into this next phase of my life, I want everyone to know the real me. I am Chelsea Manning. I am a female. Given the way that I feel, and have felt since childhood, I want to begin hormone therapy as soon as possible. I hope that you will support me in this transition. I also request that, starting today; you refer to me by my new name and use the feminine pronoun (except in official mail to the confinement facility). I look forward to receiving letters from supporters and having the opportunity to write back."

While advocacy groups GLAAD, the National Lesbian and Gay Journalists Association and the Human Rights Campaign announced their support of calling her Chelsea and using feminine pronouns, some news outlets were initially hesitant to refer to her as female.

The Today show and NBC immediately began using the feminine pronoun and referring to her as Chelsea, and by August

27, The New York Times, Associated Press, NPR, Chicago Tribune and Time Magazine had all come on board, according to an August 27, 2013, article on MSNBC.

Fox News, The National Review, Washington Times, Politico, CBS News, USA Today, Washington Post and CNN were hesitant to use Chelsea's self-identified name and pronoun, but they all came around in the coming weeks.

Eight months later in April 2014, the Kansas District Court approved Chelsea's petition for a legal name change, and the Army agreed to update the personnel records with her name change, but still treated Chelsea as a man.

Despite the fact Army physicians had diagnosed Chelsea with gender dysphoria, the Army still refused to treat her with the hormone therapy despite the fact such treatment is available in federal prisons that house civilians. The Pentagon still considered transgender persons unfit for service.

In July 2014, the Federal Bureau of Prisons rejected the Army's request to transfer Chelsea to their custody, which left her at Fort Leavenworth where she was allowed to have female undergarments. There was talk about allowing her to begin hormone treatments, but it was never clear if Manning would continue to be housed in the men's unit.

A month later, Chelsea's attorney threatened to sue the Department of Defense of they didn't allow her proper treatment for gender dysphoria. On August 22, an army spokesperson told NBC News that treatment would be provided.

"In general terms, the initial stages of treatment for individuals with gender dysphoria include psychotherapy and elements of the 'real life experience' therapy. Treatment for the condition is highly individualized and generally is sequential and graduated," the spokesperson said.

In September of that year, Chelsea's attorney filed a lawsuit against the Secretary of Defense because she had still not been permitted receive hormone therapy or grow her hair in a feminine fashion.

Chelsea, who regularly contributed to the Guardian as a mail-in columnist, spoke more about her lack of treatment and the prison's refusal to treat her.

"I filed a petition to change my name in January of this year. Even with some assistance from counsel, the petition took nearly four months to draft and file before I ever made it to a hearing before the court. The hearing and filings were public, and I had to pay fees for filing and posting a legal notice in a local newspaper costing me nearly $500. And, despite making it clear that I identify as female, and having two military psychiatrists recommend support for my transition, legally changing my name has no effect on the "legal" gender status that the government imposes upon me," she wrote in part.

Despite the Army's 2014 claims that Chelsea would receive the necessary hormone treatments, it was February 2015 before she actually received the first doses of hormones. It was the first time the Army had ever done so. Despite allowing her to utilize hormone treatment therapy, she was still forced to keep short hair.

A month later, the U.S. Army Court of Criminal Appeals agreed that Chelsea could be referred to by a feminine pronoun in future court proceedings.

"Reference to appellant in all future formal papers filed before this court and all future orders and decisions issued by this court shall either be neutral, e.g., Private First Class Manning or appellant, or employ a feminine pronoun," the ruling said.

Court documents also revealed that she had been provided with psychotherapy, hormone therapy, female undergarments, and the ability to wear some cosmetics. Chelsea wrote to Amnesty International the next month to say that she felt an "amazing relief."

"I finally began my prescribed regime of hormones to continue my overdue gender transition in February. It's been such an amazing relief for my body and brain to finally come into alignment with each other. My stress and anxiety levels have tapered off quite considerably. Overall, things are beginning to move along nicely," she told the human rights group.

Despite treatment, she was still suicidal at times. In July 2016, Chelsea passed a note to her closest friend in prison, Anthony Raby. The note was headed, "Chelsea E. Manning, re: my final letter." Chelsea had planned to kill herself once the Fourth of July fireworks display came to a close, she wrote in the letter. Fireworks had already been done for more than two hours.

Raby told the guards about the note and waited as staff responded to Chelsea's cell. It was 3:30 a.m. when they told him she was still alive.

She told the New York Times that she doesn't remember anything about the incident other than waking up in an ambulance. The few days prior to the attempt had been hard, and she was trying to wait and speak to her psychologist after the weekend.

The Washington Post reported the suicide attempt on July 5, which infuriated her attorneys. Her legal team blasted the Army for talking to the media when they wouldn't allow Chelsea to speak to her attorney for another several days.

After her recovery from the attempt, Chelsea dictated an article that was posted at Medium that she wanted to be able to define her own identity as a female.

"I admit that I want to be seen and understood as the woman that I actually am — with all of my flaws and eccentricities — perhaps at the expense of what people expect me to be," she wrote. "I hope I don't let anyone down, but it just feels better, and more honest, to reveal my boring old self."

At the end of July, the ACLU announced Chelsea was being investigating for attempting to kill herself and that she faced several charges including "resisting the force cell move team, prohibited property, and conduct which threatens." The prison would hold a disciplinary hearing for these charges, but she would not be allowed to have any representation.

On September 9, two weeks before her disciplinary hearing, she went on a hunger strike to protest what she called bullying by guards and the Army's refusal to allow her gender reassignment surgery.

The army relented on September 13, saying the surgery would proceed, though a timeline was not given. Chelsea ended her hunger strike at that time.

Her disciplinary hearing was set for September 22, and punishment for the offenses could have included indefinite solitary confinement.

Following the hearing, she was sentenced to 14 days in solitary confinement with seven to be served and seven suspended.

According to a New York Times report, Chelsea again attempted to kill herself on October 4, 2016, on her first night in solitary confinement. She hadn't been told when the stint in solitary would begin, and was blindsided by it after working in the wood shop on October 4.

The attempt landed her on suicide watch, and was placed on medical observation following her release from solitary confinement on October 11.

On October 15, while still on medical observation, she called a member of her support system to tell of what happened on the evening of Monday, October 10, 2016.

Some sources suggest the events of that night were a hallucination, a mental break from her time in confinement. Chelsea and her attorneys believe the guards staged a mock terrorist attack, prison break, kidnapping, and hostage situation in order to torment her and cause "severe psychological distress."

The person Chelsea called isn't named in the six-page report she dictated by phone and had faxed to the inspector general of the intelligence community investigations division.

According to the report, she heard two guards discussing a cyber-attack on the east coast that had killed dozens of people and cut phone access. She heard the guards say Congress had entered an emergency session to pass emergency anti-terrorism measures. There was also mention of Chelsea being "blown up" according to Twitter reports and emergency orders from Barack Obama regarding the prison at Fort Leavenworth.

In Chelsea's account, there was chaos at shift change. A woman yelled "Go Chelsea," the guards were activating their panic buttons, though they were quickly shut off. Chelsea said she heard guards asking "who are you?" and then physical fighting and shots from a piston that she believed were suppressed or silenced in some way.

The female voice began directing two other men to tie up the subdued guards and throw them in the shower. Chelsea said she saw one person bound up with zip ties.

Chelsea referred to the group as "attackers" and said they spoke to one another about bombs, maps, and escape routes.

Chelsea believed they had come to kidnap her.

"They described having clothing in the bag for 'Chelsea to wear' and wigs, sunglasses and make up. They also said 'Chelsea needs a shave,' as I had a beard and I was on suicide risk status. Several minutes passed as they harassed and seemingly tortured the injured people in the showers."

She also reported hearing some of the men speaking broken Arabic with a Saudi Arabian accent.

Chelsea said she hid in the corner of her cell, knowing that normal protocol would be to extract her from the cell. That didn't happen. She said they instead called to ask her if she was okay.

Chelsea said a guard she recognized passed her cell before breakfast, and she tried to tell him the people on the unit were just posing as guards. Instead, one of the "attackers" followed behind him, and Chelsea reported that she heard gunfire once they were out of her sight.

At breakfast, Chelsea said a tall black man she'd never seen before appeared with a container of food and Chelsea asked for the shift leader.

"The SHU (secure housing unit) shift leader is the only person authorized to give food to any inmates on suicide risk status. They normally inventory the food, item by item, in order to insure that there is a record of what the inmate eats. The 'Sergeant' responded that, 'Oh, he couldn't make it,'" she said.

Chelsea refused breakfast and said the shift change occurred again at 6 a.m.

"Everything returned to normal, except that several correctional specialists were "deep cleaning" the entirety of Alpha tier with Pine Sol and bleach," she said.

The Army told the New York Times that the event was a complete fabrication. A psychiatrist called it a "mistake" to subject Chelsea to isolation given her fragile mental state, and said such a hallucination is common in people who are in solitary confinement.

Attorneys for Chelsea reported in December 2016 that the army doctor treating her was refusing to change her gender on her military records to female, a move that was not explained at the time. Chelsea was quoted in the New York Times in January 2017, just before Barack Obama commuted her sentence, that she still hadn't seen a surgeon.

In a tweet in early July 2017, she responded to a critic complaining about the use of taxpayer funds to help pay for her transition surgery. She replied that the government had paid only $600 for hormone replacement medication during her incarceration.

Free Chelsea

Chelsea's attorney immediately began trying to get her pardoned following her sentencing hearing in 2013.

First, Coombs filed a petition for pardon/commutation. The petition, which used masculine pronouns despite Chelsea's announcement, said the documents hadn't caused any damage and weren't sensitive.

Amnesty International said Chelsea was more of a whistleblower, saying that her leak had revealed human rights violations.

In April 2014, the request for clemency was denied and the case advanced to the Army Court of Criminal Appeals.

Amnesty International posted a letter from her in April 2015. She sounded upbeat about the appeal.

"I am now preparing for my court-martial appeal before the first appeals court. The appeal team, with my attorneys Nancy Hollander and Vince Ward, are hoping to file our brief before the court in the next six months. We have already had success in getting the court to respect my gender identity by using feminine pronouns in the court filings (she, her, etc.)," she wrote.

In November 2016, Chelsea and her attorneys again petitioned the president, but this time they asked for her sentence to be commuted to time served.

The 27-page petition included a seven-page statement from Chelsea herself.

She said she knew her request for a pardon was too much too soon after being sentenced.

"Sitting here today I understand why the petition was not acted on. It was too soon, and the requested relief was too much. I should have waited. I needed time to absorb the conviction, and to reflect on my actions. I also needed time to grow and mature as a person."

She said she still needed more intensive treatment for her gender dysphoria and said the length of her sentence was unprecedented compared to the sentences of other leakers.

"I have served a sufficiently long sentence. I am not asking for a pardon of my conviction. I understand that the various collateral consequences of the court-martial conviction will stay on my record forever. The sole relief I am asking for is to be released from military prison after serving six years of confinement as a person who did not intend to harm the interests of the United States or harm any service members," she said in part. "I am merely asking for a first chance to live my life outside the USDB as the person I was born to be."

Her petition also featured letters of support from United States Air Force Colonel Morris

D. Davis, Ret., who asked the president to reduce Chelsea's sentence to 10 years instead of 35.

"I urge you to grant clemency by reducing PFC Manning's sentence to 10 years, which still sends a strong deterrent message consistent with good order and discipline in the armed forces," Morris wrote.

Daniel Ellsberg, who released the Pentagon Papers in 1971, also voiced his support for Chelsea. He asked that she be released immediately.

"There is no doubt that these six years have been devastating to a person who sought nothing more than to inform the American public. She sought no personal gain from her disclosures," Ellsberg wrote.

On the outside, there was an entire movement of support to try and encourage Obama to free Chelsea which only ramped up following the election of Donald Trump.

A petition to the White House asking for a commutation reached the 100,000 signature threshold to elicit an official response.

Lawyers who studied Obama's clemency and pardon-granting techniques told Politico in December that Chelsea getting any kind of relief was unlikely. The administration typically shied away from high-profile cases.

Yet six weeks after the White House petition reached its goal, Obama announced that Chelsea would be freed.

Chelsea was granted a commutation just three days before President Barack Obama left office.

"It has been my view that given she went to trial, that due process was carried out, that she took responsibility for her crime … and that she had served a significant amount of time," Obama said on January 18, 2017. "That it makes sense to commute – and not pardon – her sentence."

When she got the news, she was in the prison workshop, covered in wood shavings after a bit of work. She told the New York

Times she was terrified when she saw security personnel enter the room. She assumed she would be sent back to solitary confinement.

Instead, she saw CNN playing on a television.

Her sentence had been commuted.

Adrian Lamo was quick to respond on Twitter. "I remain confident in my 2010 decision. In that time and circumstance, it was needful. It was cold, but it had to be made then and there," he said.

He went on to post an article on Medium saying Chelsea had suffered, and he surmised that commuting her sentence was to save her from suicide, calling it a death penalty she was not sentenced to.

"She committed a crime, and society deserved to have that crime punished. It has been. Perhaps more so than it needed to be. I don't know. All I can say for sure is that I'm closing the book on this chapter of my life, as Chelsea opens another. I played my role, as did many people," Lamo wrote.

Chelsea's release date was set for May 17, 2017 almost 7 years to the day since the military's criminal investigation division arrested her at FOB Hammer in Iraq.

Today

Chelsea was released from Fort Leavenworth around 2 a.m. on May 17, 2017. She was loaded into an SUV and taken to meet two attorneys.

Her first tweet as a free woman was a photo of her feet and legs adorned in black Converse shows and black leggings. She captioned it, "First Steps of Freedom" around 10 a.m. that morning. Two and a half hours later, she tweeted a photo of a slice of pizza.

Her supporters already had her taken care of long before her release from prison. A GoFundMe campaign rose well over $100,000 that was released to Chelsea when she left prison. The funds were raised to "pay for Chelsea's rent, utilities, health care, clothing and other living expenses for the first year after she is released," the GoFundMe page said.

Chelsea maintains an active Twitter account with several tweets each day where she interacts with some of her 245,000 followers. She began tweeting in 2013 by way of phone calls to supporters.

In April 2015, Chelsea had those supporters post a handwritten letter to her Twitter account to douse rumors that the account was fake.

"I wanted to set up this account a while ago, but I didn't really have the energy to until I began to start taking hormones a few months ago. So a few weeks ago I asked my friend [name] if he would set up an account that I reserved in 2013, and he agreed to help me at no cost," she wrote in part. "The tweets, except for retweets, are verbatim dictation over the phone to someone that I can call from here in Kansas."

Chelsea will likely continue writing for the Guardian, a task she took on in February 2015 when she became a contributing columnist on the topics of gender, war, and freedom of information. It was an unpaid gig, but her articles garnered thousands of shared as they appeared throughout her incarceration. As of early July 2017, she has not written another opinion piece since February 2017.

Chelsea lives in New York City and she found an agent, who is trying to sell her memoir to a publishing house. She finished the 300-page manuscript during her last few months at Fort Leavenworth.

A documentary about her, XY Chelsea, is set to air this fall. Xychelsea is also her Twitter handle.

Chelsea gave several interviews following her release from prison. She spoke to ABC's Good Morning America that she and she alone was responsible for the release of the documents. She gave a lengthy interview to the New York Times to discuss her entire ordeal.

She is still very active on Twitter, her words decorated with emojis as she fends off other users who call her at traitor and tell her she should still be in prison.

As of July 2017, Chelsea is still on active duty status with the Army, though she's on "voluntary excess leave" meaning she has not been discharged and is not being paid, but the Army would have the jurisdiction to charge her if she stepped out of line in any way. She is still expected to abide by the uniform code of military justice as long as she is considered a member of the armed services.

She continues to appeal her court-martial convictions.

Printed in Great Britain
by Amazon